WITHDRAWN
FROM COLLECTION

PLUTO

The Icy Dwarf Planet

by Chaya Glaser

Consultant: Karly M. Pitman, PhD
Planetary Science Institute
Tucson, Arizona

BEARPORT PUBLISHING

New York, New York

Credits
Cover, © NASA/APL; TOC, © Friedrich Saurer/Science Source; 4–5, © Detlev van Ravenswaay/Science Source; 6–7, © Wikipedia & NASA; 8–9, © NASA; 8, © Friedrich Saurer/Science Source; 10, © NASA/SDO (AIA); 11, © Friedrich Saurer/Science Source; 12, © NASA; 13, © Lee Prince/Shutterstock; 14–15, © ESO/L. Calcada; 16–17, © Walter Myers/Science Source; 18–19, © Chris Butler/Science Source; 20–21, © Johns Hopkins University Applied Physics Laboratory/Southwest Research Institute; 23TL, © Chris Butler/Science Photo Library; 23TR, © Wikipedia & NASA; 23BL, © Wikipedia & NASA; 23BR, © Johns Hopkins University Applied Physics Laboratory/Southwest Research Institute.

Publisher: Kenn Goin
Editor: Jessica Rudolph
Creative Director: Spencer Brinker
Design: Debrah Kaiser
Photo Researcher: Michael Win

Library of Congress Cataloging-in-Publication Data

Glaser, Chaya, author.
  Pluto : The Icy Dwarf Planet / by Chaya Glaser.
      pages cm. — (Out of this world)
  Includes bibliographical references and index.
  ISBN 978-1-62724-571-5 (library binding) — ISBN 1-62724-571-5 (library binding)
  1. Pluto (Dwarf planet)—Juvenile literature. I. Title.
  QB701.G53 2015
  523.49'22—dc23
                                    2014040706

For more information, write to Bearport Publishing Company, Inc., 45 West 21st Street, Suite 3B, New York, New York 10010. Printed in the United States of America.

10 9 8 7 6 5 4 3 2 1

CONTENTS

What's the most famous dwarf planet?

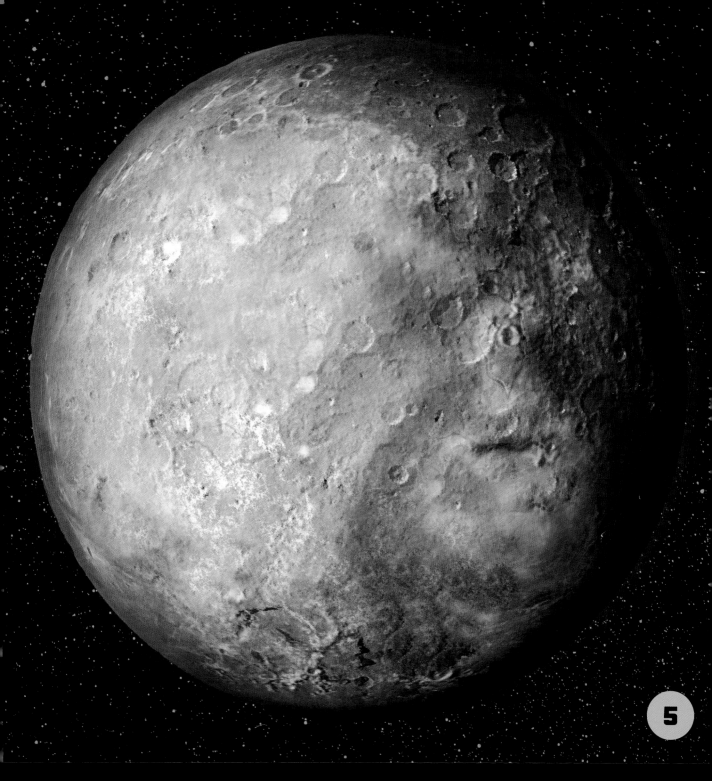

5

Pluto is part of Earth's Solar System.

JUPITER

MARS

VENUS

EARTH

MERCURY

SUN

6

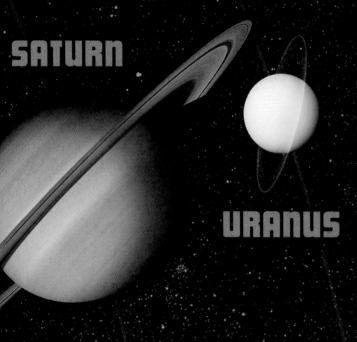

SATURN

NEPTUNE

URANUS

PLUTO

It orbits, or moves
around, the Sun.

Years ago, Pluto was called a planet, like Earth and Saturn.

PLUTO

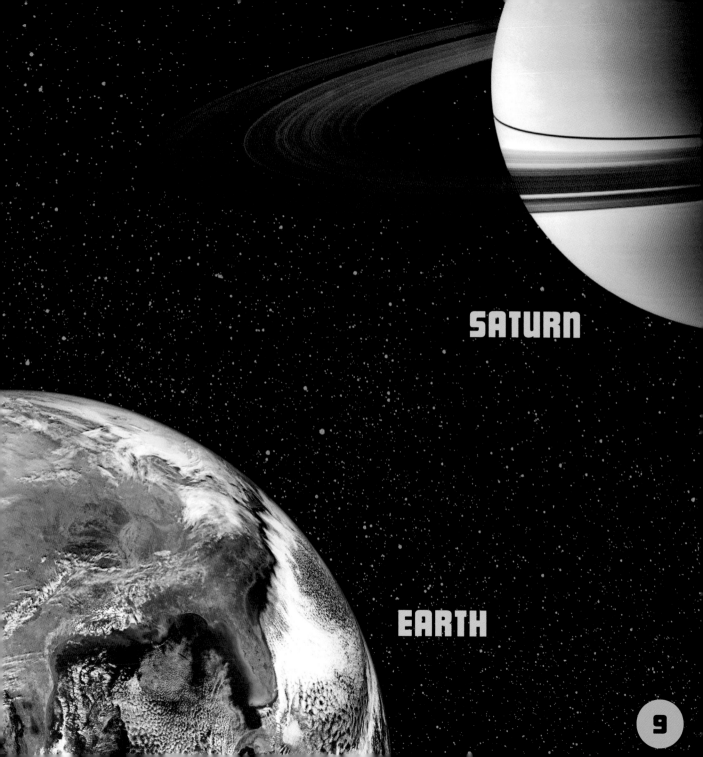

SATURN

EARTH

9

Now scientists call Pluto a dwarf planet.

WHY?

PLUTO

It is very small.

Pluto is much smaller than Earth.

It is even smaller than the smallest planet—Mercury.

PLUTO

MERCURY

EARTH

In fact, 166 Plutos could fit inside Earth!

Pluto is very far from the Sun.

Little heat and light reach it.

The dwarf planet is cold
and dark.

PLUTO

It is covered with rock and ice.

sun

15

There are many other
dwarf planets.

PLUTO

HAUMEA

ERIS

Some are located
near Pluto.

Five moons orbit Pluto.

18

Scientists believe there are more moons to discover.

Pluto's largest moon, Charon

In 2006, a **spacecraft** left Earth to explore Pluto.

It will take many years to get there.

The spacecraft may discover new dwarf planets near Pluto!

PLUTO

A spacecraft

PLUTO VERSUS EARTH

PLUTO	VERSUS	EARTH
Beyond Neptune, the eighth planet from the Sun	POSITION	Third planet from the Sun
1,471 miles (2,367 km) across	SIZE	7,918 miles (12,743 km) across
About −378°F (−228°C)	AVERAGE TEMPERATURE	59°F (15°C)
Five	NUMBER OF MOONS	One
Rock and ice	SURFACE	Mostly oceans, some land

GLOSSARY

dwarf planet (DWORF PLAN-it)   an object in space that orbits the Sun and is smaller than a planet

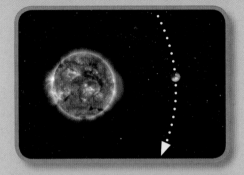

orbits (OR-bits)   circles around a planet, the Sun, or another object

Solar System (SOH-lur SISS-tuhm)   the Sun and everything that circles around it, including eight large planets and many dwarf planets

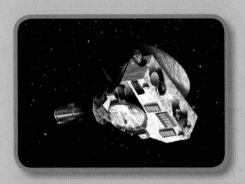

spacecraft (SPAYSS-kraft)   a vehicle that can travel in space

INDEX

READ MORE

Landau, Elaine. *Pluto: From Planet to Dwarf (True Book).* New York: Children's Press (2008).

Lawrence, Ellen. *Pluto and the Dwarf Planets (Zoom Into Space).* New York: Ruby Tuesday Books (2014).

LEARN MORE ONLINE

To learn more about Pluto, visit
www.bearportpublishing.com/OutOfThisWorld

ABOUT THE AUTHOR

Chaya Glaser enjoys looking up at the stars and reading stories about the constellations. When she's not admiring the night sky, she can be found playing musical instruments.